W9-DEL-064

A Door
to the Shore

Jan Westberg

Consulting Editor, Diane Craig, M.A./Reading Specialist

Published by ABDO Publishing Company, 4940 Viking Drive, Edina, Minnesota 55435.

Printed in the United States.

Credits
Edited by: Pam Price
Curriculum Coordinator: Nancy Tuminelly
Cover and Interior Design and Production: Mighty Media
Photo Credits: BananaStock Ltd., Brand X Pictures, Comstock, Corbis Images, Corel, Hemera, Image 100, Image Source, PhotoDisc, Stockbyte

Library of Congress Cataloging-in-Publication Data

Westberg, Jan.
    A door to the shore / Jan Westberg.
       p. cm. -- (Rhyme time)
    ISBN 1-59197-786-X
    1. English language--Rhyme--Juvenile literature. I. Title. II. Rhyme time (ABDO Publishing Company)

    PE1517.W477 2004
    808.1--dc22
                                                              2004049038

SandCastle™ books are created by a professional team of educators, reading specialists, and content developers around five essential components that include phonemic awareness, phonics, vocabulary, text comprehension, and fluency. All books are written, reviewed, and leveled for guided reading, early intervention reading, and Accelerated Reader® programs and designed for use in shared, guided, and independent reading and writing activities to support a balanced approach to literacy instruction.

Let Us Know

After reading the book, SandCastle would like you to tell us your stories about reading. What is your favorite page? Was there something hard that you needed help with? Share the ups and downs of learning to read. We want to hear from you! To get posted on the ABDO Publishing Company Web site, send us e-mail at:

sandcastle@abdopub.com

SandCastle Level: Transitional

Words that rhyme do not have to be spelled the same. These words rhyme with each other:

before

explore

boar

floor

chore

for

door

shore

drawer

store

Aidan is taller than he was before.

The big boar stands in a field.

Raking leaves is Britta's favorite chore.

Taylor and Jules pose with their parents outside their front **door**.

Shawn and Laurence think
the library is a great place
to **explore**.

The cat likes to sleep in
the **drawer**.

Miguel and his family run along the shore.

Geoff and Kent are playing on the **floor**.

Darla's mother helps her pick out clothes at the **store**.

Cindy and Fran study together for their history test.

A Door
to the Shore

John and I went to Baltimore
to visit John's uncle, Mr. Voor.

Mr. Voor has a special store,
filled with treasures from ceiling to floor.

When we arrived, Mr. Voor
was counting the cash in the drawer.
He said, "You go ahead and explore.
I will join you when I finish this chore."

We ran off to explore the store
and way in back saw a purple door.

We asked, "Mr. Voor,
what is that purple door for?"

He said, "You were too young
when you were here before,
but now it's time you learned
about the purple door."

He threw open the door,
and there was the shore!

We spent the day surfing
and built sandcastles galore.

We were glad
that the door to the shore
was secret no more!

Rhyming Riddle

What do you call a job for a male pig?

Boar chore

Glossary

boar. a male pig

chore. a regular job or task, like cleaning your room

explore. to investigate or examine

galore. in abundance or in large quantities

shore. the land at the edge of an ocean or lake

About SandCastle™

A professional team of educators, reading specialists, and content developers created the SandCastle™ series to support young readers as they develop reading skills and strategies and increase their general knowledge. The SandCastle™ series has four levels that correspond to early literacy development in young children. The levels are provided to help teachers and parents select the appropriate books for young readers.

Emerging Readers
(no flags)

Beginning Readers
(1 flag)

Transitional Readers
(2 flags)

Fluent Readers
(3 flags)

These levels are meant only as a guide. All levels are subject to change.

ABDO
Publishing Company

To see a complete list of SandCastle™ books and other nonfiction titles from ABDO Publishing Company, visit www.abdopub.com or contact us at:
4940 Viking Drive, Edina, Minnesota 55435 • 1-800-800-1312 • fax: 1-952-831-1632